The Rabbits Could Sing

Other Books in the Alaska Literary Series

Peggy Shumaker, series editor

The City Beneath the Snow, by Marjorie Kowalski Cole (short stories)
The Cormorant Hunter's Wife, by Joan Kane (poetry)

The Rabbits Could Sing

poems by

Amber Flora Thomas

ALASKA
LITERARY
SERIES

University of Alaska Press
Fairbanks

University of Alaska Press
P.O. Box 756240
Fairbanks, AK 99775-6240

Alaska Literary Series

Library of Congress Cataloging-in-Publication Data

Thomas, Amber Flora.
The rabbits could sing : poems / Amber Flora Thomas.
p. cm. — (Alaska literary series)
ISBN 978-1-60223-159-7 (pbk. : acid-free paper)
ISBN 978-1-60223-160-3 (electronic book)
I. Title.
PS3620.H6246R33 2012
811'.6—dc23
2011032943

Cover and interior design by Andrew Mendez
Cover illustration *Morning Gathering*, © 2010 by Raya
This publication was printed on acid-free paper that meets the minimum
requirements for ANSI / NISO Z39.48–1992 (R2002)
(Permanence of Paper for Printed Library Materials).

Acknowledgments

I would like to thank the following journals and anthologies where these poems first appeared, many in earlier versions.

Alaska Quarterly Review: "Cavity in the Rubenesque Façade," "Ultrasound Aubade," and "Meditation on Four West"; *American Literary Review*: "After"; *Bloom*: "Bull Frog" and "Hood"; *Borderlands: Texas Poetry Review*: "The Chipped Bowl" and "Girl in the Woods" (previously titled "A Response to What I Do Not Know"); *Callaloo*: "Swarm," "The Killed Rabbit," and "Killing the Rabbit: Ars Poetica"; *Carolina Quarterly*: "Self-Portrait in the Tide"; *Cloud View Poets: Anthology from the Master Classes of David St. John* (Arctos Press): "The Chipped Bowl"; *The Comstock Review*: "Regarding Mercy" and "Heart with Interior View"; *Crab Orchard Review*: "The Killed Rabbit," "Migraine Confessional," "Unattended" (previously titled "Unattended Prayer"), and "The Get Away"; *Hunger Mountain*: "Killing the Rabbit: Ars Poetica"; *In Posse Review* online journal: "Conversation with the Sculptor" and "Braid"; *New Poets of the American West* (Many Voices Press): "Swarm"; *Orion Magazine*: "Black Dog"; *Pedestal* online journal: "Magician" and "Serenade"; *PMS poemmemoirstory*: "Swarm" and "Dear Reader"; *PEN American Center – Beyond Black History Month Poetry Relay online*: "Girl in the Woods," Conversation with the Sculptor," "Hood," and "Killing the Rabbit: Ars Poetica"; *RHINO*: "Spider"; *Rosebud Magazine*: "When You Rise You Do Not Drown"; *RUNES, A Review of Poetry*: "Prayer Found in Water Pouring Down a Bus Window"; *Spillway Magazine*: "April Spill-Off"; *Writing Self and Community: African American Poetry after the Civil Rights Movement* (W. W. Norton): "Swarm" and "The Killed Rabbit"; *ZYZZYVA*: "Then You Fled the Room".

I would like to thank the following organizations for their generous support during the completion of this manuscript: Alaska State Council for the Arts, the Corporation of Yaddo, Atlantic Center for the Arts, and the Cave Canem Foundation.

Thank you to *Crab Orchard Review* for awarding me the Richard Peterson Poetry Prize for a group of poems from this book.

Thank you to *Rosebud Magazine* for awarding me the Dylan Thomas American Poet Prize for "When You Rise You Do Not Drown."

Also, much thanks to Susan Terris for her guidance in the compilation of this work.

Table of Contents

I

II

—For my father

The Rabbits Could Sing

I

In August

Reading the Sunday news, another bomb
has gone off in a Baghdad marketplace,
we have killed twelve grizzlies
in Alaska's Interior—yesterday's caught
in a pigpen finishing a second sow:
a tiny morsel to her 1,400 pounds.

I cradle a red apple in my fist. My dog
rests her head on my thigh. She too
likes a crisp bite of apple; streams of juice
burst between my teeth. No mushy flesh
too long waiting in a grocer's bin.
No air under the skin or white worm
squirming out of a black core.

The thick skin cracks with a cider's maul—
a good, good bite for which there is never enough,
and sweet still to suck the pulp. When I have
gnawed all the way to the core, a seed
pops from a firm cell and lulls in my mouth.

I ruffle my dog's sleek brown ears.
It is a dream I tell myself. I am free, yes,
and reading the news in August
and eating a red apple.

Swarm

A honeybee queen lays the nettle
and the weather in a black cloud that falls
on two white men lifting a rotten tree
toward their truck on the fire road. It's just luck

come up from hiding, a nether world
she sends into the August groan. The men hack
and flail pale limber arms at the air, their clothing,
and their ears. They jig around the truck
in this unexpected season.

I stand alone across the gully and kill
the helpful girl trying to rise up
in me. If they had found me alone
on my afternoon walk in the forest?

Their baseball caps shucked, the red rising
on their arms and faces. The bees go up
and come down, a dizzy swarm. The men
throw themselves into the cab of the truck,

the haze ascending on their dust, until
nothing they could have done was done to me.

To a Reader

I have a silver canoe you might want,
quicksand from my dream last night,
two tickets to Sydney, and a river
a mile wide, the bounty that knows
my crimes and hunts me like a dog.

I have a papier-mâché woman
that says, "Tell you
your fortune?" and offers
the Two of Swords every time.

I have the last fifteen minutes
of my sleep, a highway in my mind's eye
and a hitchhiker thumbing the air.
I have surgeries and doctors and
three hundred vials of fool's gold, and I
can go no farther south.

Watch me collide with the 1970s again
and bad B-movies, interrogating
a Jell-O substance bubbling out of
the sink drain. I have exiled
photographs of bruised children
and a predisposition for praise.

I have picked you a gallon of cranberries,
tart to taste. When the past slips over
the field like a red dress, I lie down
in the tundra on this mountain pass
and belong to the sky again.

The Chipped Bowl

A woman carries a basket into a field.
She represents someone's eternity
in blue-and-white China. It's fall there
and two geese travel toward a pond.

She does not know her destination
has become an abyss into your day—
American headlines on the newspaper,
a cat lazing in a sunny rectangle by the stove.

The story of where she would arrive
broken away, its lip weathered brown. She will not
go to a hut with a thatched roof, or to a willow
and idyll beneath its drowsy branches.

She will always be on the verge of her life
with her carved bone buttons, her bonnet.
She will never know if there is burlap
or velvet. How long will she carry her basket
into the absence beyond the field?

You have grown accustomed
to the shattered image of her tranquil
ascent into your day, and the falseness
of her story, no matter how you end it.
You eat of this longing.

Take Off the Yellow Slicker

The wasp's body brings the cracking all up my leg.
My shoe holds the danger to the floor

until I am sure. I am no flower, "no wilting lily,"
as someone said years ago. Weapons surround my house:

idiot traps with poisonous meats into which they fly
and cannot escape. Good soldiers of a summer daze.

The window screens only partially filter the raid.
The cracking goes all up my leg, a small shiver

when I draw back. The shell recoils into the integrity of sleep,
fetal and wet on the linoleum; it is easy to let the battle in.

Three Windows

It is to make her merely literary. To write:
"Her hand grips the mattress where the sheet
has sprung from its corner." To give the girl a job
while thinking is a torrential welling, and she ricochets
farther into that dark. I've had enough of her
lilting, enough carrying her, speechless and torn, in
and out of my decades. I say: "She sits up,

pulls her dress over her head, and buckles
her sandals." The writer works with the bare room,
with beer bottles lined up below a window, and pigeons
that flit and press their sleep to the ledge outside.
The writer hears a garbage truck in the alley,
a car barely through a red light.

I say: "The girl pushes a barrette in her brown hair.
She walks to the door, the brass knob fitting coolly
against her palm as she twists its bulbous head."
I work her literary edges and say: "She felt a reed
bend along her throat and this fat brown tongue
spoke an airy lament to the morning." The writer

goes back to refine the pigeons' sleep, knocks over
a green bottle, and pulls the city open in morning traffic.
"The girl walks to the elevator and pushes the arrow 'down.'
She digs in her purse for a number, a comb." I say: "Her soul
from flight, her swallowing, and her not remembering
the night hours, so they will loosen over her
for years." The writer remembers the newspaper

folded on the nightstand and an ashtray with
eight cigarette butts smashed into the brown glass
bottom. The pigeons coo on the ledge outside.
Later, she remembers the naked girl inside the room,
not yet the writer and writing, though prolific,
leaving red roses everywhere she had lain.

Migraine Confessional

I've been seeing cubist all day,
the human shape a hazard,
assuming too much light.

Your lips a piece. Your tongue
an instrument of static.
I hear expulsions. I can't speak.

My temples hold sound verbatim:
ocean, ocean and sea grass,
wind rush.

Sun heat in my lap. Point of light
or point of dark—the fault eddies
between my eyes. Seeing won't let up:

a white bird thrashing. I've got to
name the ghost something other than
tide. I am pulled into breakage

and out of a wave a woman whirls
in a red dress, fluid shimmy
holding her temples.

When You Rise You Do Not Drown

He is laughing: his laughter
when a hummingbird pauses, buzzing
at the sweat on his forehead.
I am waking underwater.

I come back to shore, gasping,
nasal passages burning from water
the wrong way in. He catches me again,
a red-backed crab scurrying onto the beach,
and I sail through cold and green
until I have fists full of sand.

Sometimes there are no birds in a field.
The fish must cut the surface to flee the net.
The tire caught by a rope and tied
to the highest branch in an oak
swings.

Before God and cornbread,
until I love every last pea: his laughter.
He says a lion shakes the sun out
and it will be summer always.

The surface pours off my gaze
and I chomp at the air, that copious room
inside my chest filling with thunder.
I am swimming.

Serenade

The doe sings when you have her by the ears,
like a bow drawn over violin strings wrong.

Mother splits celery stalks and onions
into crisp chunks for the stew.

In the morning you found the doe eating her litter,
snacking on fine pink ears and hairless bodies
trampled against the cage wire. Bad rabbit.

She sings like the broken violin in her belly
can still give her Vivaldi for her only aria.

Her song eats hillsides and roads, churns in the ears of neighbors,
slipping over rattlesnake sounds coming from weeds.

No more wheezing breath or rattling the cage doors,
when you find a way into her body.
You are a magician

and she breaks out of her skin for you. Is this a good ending?
Mother drops the okra and garlic in the pot.

We taste the promise coming forward to bid her passage:
a necessary eternity of feasts.

Woman on Shore

The current talks around her legs; her white skirt
held above her knees, sailing the distortion.

She sees herself ripple from muse to doll,
not a sensible human shape, whirling with each new force,
so all is known across and separate, too.

Beneath the surface the current hangs up,
changes its course. A fishing line
tangled on some rocks at her feet
gathers algae with its baited yellow hook;
minnows scatter to her ankles.

The river unfolds and sends motion away from shore.
Someone on the beach calls to her and she turns and smiles,
a few hairs clinging to her lips. And then

a dog leaps after a stick crushing water like it is
merely air trained in resistance. He runs on nothing
but the hurt to taste wood again.

Penny's Gallon

We settle on the porch to discuss the rumor.
She has had five husbands and all of them
dead; the last one, ashes buried in a gallon-size
mayonnaise jar beneath an oak in the yard.

We stare at the oak's broad trunk. We stare at the day
ending, flies converse in her arm hair. She says
she digs him up sometimes "to be sure." His dust
held apart from the rich earth, not so heavy
that the genie couldn't leap from his bottle.

She offers me bourbon and a turkey & swiss
on whole wheat. She says you have to need it bad,
and strokes down her wrist, blue veins.

I don't want to miss my train, though
her poodle won't let me go and hops in my lap,
tinkles a little when I say, "Good boy."

Who eats a gallon of mayonnaise in a year,
let alone ten years? How long would it take
to finish such a glob, how many sandwiches
and salads? My stomach twists. I can't get away
from death. It's about to spell my name
on the chipped white porch.

"I'll miss my train," I say.
"I'll see you next time," I say.
And there are the deep sad lines in her smile
some men have loved themselves against.

Summer Mold

No queens, but spores until I can barely breathe
in those legions. I move the bookcase and find
thin black arms stretching across the paint.

Then a door opens: upon, once, fairy tale,
a crude start to the journey, wishes to disperse.
I look and look, like one reading tea leaves,
legs folded on the floor. I come to a dark wood

and walk into the night, as if plenty of stale bread
fills my pockets, and will at last offer a way out,
or through. I go back to writing, a woman
gazing from her tower window, suspended,
and patient for what will (and maybe never) arrive.

The forest has joined me in the writing room.
Tomorrow the landlord will bring buckets of bleach water
and scrub a not quite blank canvas in its place.

II

Listen

A man trimming his fingernails on a park bench.
He gazes at the white edge of each crown: *clip, clip.*
He brushes a hand over his pant leg, slivers
land in the grass. Listen for what comes next
and what came before. The wind carries a plastic bag
that shimmies pink among some leaves. Touch
your rough edges: snag. Dishes, garden soil, teeth
put to worry. You miss the jolts from thinking,
easy repercussions of a robin ladling song from a branch,
the *Hello* spilling across the street. Listen: water
unable to excuse rock in a fountain, a child spanks
the surface. A dog stretches his neck on the tight end of a rope.

Conversation with the Sculptor

It's the way my father made a body
out of knots. The sculpted metal heads
with eyes sewn open and ears wired back
grew numerous in my childhood.

Heads perched on pedestals, brain stems
growing dusty denominations, fascinating lint.
My thinking used up by the greatest thinkers.

Infinite, far beyond me, their metal mouths
forming a logic my father's pliers clamped
and bent into place.

The past spirals out of me. Static.
I'm no longer pouring out apologies.
I mumble my truce with bones, tendons,
words quick to leave my tongue.

Does he see the doves I keep between
my shoulder blades, almost breaking gray wings
when they burst from my mouth, hell to pay
as they catapult into the sky?

Self-Portrait in the Tide

I write myself onto the ark: going up the stairs
toward the apartment with two bags of groceries.

My wife is in there. Oh yes, I am her . . .
about to make dinner, choosing stasis in the tide,
a current sabotaged by wind. Dolphins somersault

inside me. I can make a whole ocean
out of my clutches, bring all the necessities to the door.
I will be released from the famine.

I hold the key to the lock like I'm holding out an iris.
Someone take my hand, this flower
though we are water.

I staunch the paper with poorly spelled words:
the boat that comes to get me.

Come in from the Sky

A cathedral waited in my mind
as I leaned over her mouth.
The shelves around us spilled
casebooks, encyclopedias, dictionaries.
I repeated the doctrine: a man should not
lay down with his neighbor's wife.
Her dildo's curved beak glistened
as it left my body.

The curfew on my flood
of shame was punctuated by her moan.
I heard a chorus in her throat, the bird's ribs
snapping against her palate. She might have
spoken if not for my kiss, the fat sound
rolling around in my mouth like a jaw-
breaker: affirmed, allowed.

Had praise been the clitoris's silky crown
and not a bud of oak or elm.
Had the hymns been practiced by shaky
woman tongues we put each into each,
I would have sheltered here.

Black Dog

Loan me your best shovel. I will dig the hole.
This earth is soft. I kick it with my boot
and it chips up. See, the hole is already started.

The dog wants to go in the ground.
He dug that hole in his yard until his chain
would let him no deeper.

I am good with death. Let me show you
with this hole. I won't let it be too shallow.
I will have him in the ground before dark.

Make supper, switch on the porch light for me.
The other dogs will gladly eat his share.
This is where he was going.
This is what was down there.

Killing the Rabbit: Ars Poetica

You have to hit it on the head with a hammer,
good and hard between the ears. You will think
of hunger, as its tongue preens its wet nose
and its legs buck air and its eyes roll back
into its skull. You have to think of killing

as a kind of weather: you make the fewest incisions
and bleed the body, slipping your hand
into the chest cavity so the innards come free
and the whole skin can be peeled off.

You'll want to make use of the lean shell
and ignore the gut pile. You won't mind black flies
buzzing over your work; you are used to critics.

You will want heaven and hell, celestial certainties
that the soul may travel into mercy.

You will think a long time about how the creature
does not cry out.

You will bring the knife into your sleep.
You will hear the cries in your dreaming. You will think
about the tenderness of the killer: hands excavating the cavity,
holding open the animal so our eyes can get in.

Thinking in Front of a Mirror

Flimsy breath, have you come to speak
for her body? She calls you November
with so much absence tending the days.

Rain this morning after rain all night,
and still, images drop their dry leaves
into the sea of her.

The hollow beyond her kiss, you asked
to be the subject of her form.

The answers given to her arrive like accidents.
She turns the crystal knob and water whines on.
The hair falls through her fingers. She glances
out a window to where a man chops wood,
stops, and throws a stick for her dog.

She cups her palms and holds her face
in the tepid pool, she does not give up on seeing
herself. Not seeing herself
is a form of your disappearance.

Era of a Happy Heart

It was a marriage of August and dirty dishes.
A moth settled for three days on the wall behind the bed.

I brought my eyes into the room of her eyes.
I came away with black brown heather muslin dust.

I said, "Now I'm going to undress you."
I washed against a creature of air.

The ceiling spoke a trick of wood knots, changing
scripture of the slope. I wondered about a life spent alone.

For hours a violin played down the hall. I said, "Look,
a hundred black birds rising in unison."

The mind of sadness was unified flight,
the aerodynamics of the flock in a neighboring field.

The dogs in the valley tore the silence open
for a passing fox. Her breath fasted on dream.

I came away with black brown heather muslin dust.
Shadows stole knowledge of her in their disposal of the day.

Biology Lesson

Don't tell anybody what you find
when the scalpel's in there: your tongue
or the ripple of birds leaving a river.

Do I wing to your thigh? This is the fly
in the throat, when your fingers open on my breasts,
the reason we must build trellises
in a decade of chalk.

I blunder with your arms around me,
a scaffolding's temporary embrace. Thought waits for me
like an ax, ready to strike a log
that houses a hive of yellow jackets, too late
when your solidness races into consciousness.

I'll be late for study hall. Yet, here is
the cystic ruby, feathery and slick gem,
that you name a heart. The waves demand
bubbling sand. The birds have scattered
against the sky.

The fishers of feeling are locked down
to the page. The hive rises to meet
the disassembled need. I underline a passage,
put a note in the margin: "always return."

Here

I call your body *home* and listen
for all the rooms I'll occupy,
the brag of my heels on marble,
a curtain's steady notes,
tonguing the wall.

It's a dizzy prayer
I bend into you and find
the thief with her hand
in the silverware drawer.

Red silk poppies anchor a web
by the door. The postman passes
at three, sorting the day's news.
The light goes divvying up
dust motes.

I don't swim away from
the greedy snapping of breath,
but my throat . . . well,
terror owns each kiss.

Collarbone, you belong to my lips.
Belly, I have a palm you may push
your tremble against.

And later, silence is a trophy
in every room, owning the days
with its crumpled sheets and
many, many questions.

More Light Because Her Shadow Shook

This morning I see myself in a mirror
above the café bar. I see myself look away.
In my cup, coffee bubbles bitter foam.
Bob Marley serenades, "No woman, no cry."
No clouds, but a hawk circling two hundred feet up,
so as not to cast its shadow on the field mouse.

A man at the next bench smiles his rotten teeth
before sucking the last of his Marlboro in, says
"Thirty percent chance of rain means no rain."

The counter help yells, "Mocha whip." Marley warns us,
"In this bright future, you can't forget your past."
I remember with my thighs what a tongue is.
A topless girl tattooed on a brown shoulder passes by.
I dig a smooth agate from my pocket and hold
its ether to the sun—reverberating stars in there.

A mother pushing a child
Balances a muffin on a paper plate.
A hornet gives one last hiss at the glass
and zips into traffic. The hawk at fifty feet
still keeps its shadow to the side.

In the Georgia O'Keeffe Museum

A swollen hive opens its fluttering eye.
My gaze slides over ten unnamed cities.
So many people not to think about,
so many countries of thought
where I cannot take refuge.

My shoes stopped on the viewing line;
the guard is ready with a warning.
I lean toward gold-framed petals
and wade into red cannas.

I would burn your letters again,
unsettled your vases, my face
and mouth full of your weather.
I am exalted by the same notes
the pianist plays in the lobby.

Across the room, heels snap the floor up.
I'm undoing your sashes again, lowering
your skirt. Into the rushes, up against
the veins and dew, I press my mouth;
horses canter into the red wake.

Membrane

I stare through silver bubble burst, less and less with air,
arms sidestroking to keep me treading beneath
the river longer. Blurry instances of sound
choke my ears. Sun splinters the green surface.

Your brown hair and my black hair finger currents,
both of us Medusas. I laugh my last breath out,
swallow water, and must rise, gasping back the air.
I have lost to a head full of snakes!

Kids building sandcastles on the shore want
their turn with the orange bucket. A radio drums
the eye of the tiger. A teenager cannonballs off a rock;
I wait for the tide to rush across my shoulders.

You spring from the cool depths, satisfied triumph
beside me. Fingers drawn across your eyes
free beading water from your lashes. Yes,
you need less than me. Yes, your greater patience
for what you cannot have.

You gulp air in and laugh after the joke is over.
I already understand what it is to be in the world without you.

After

Two Appaloosas come from deep
in their field to take crab apples
from my palm, ears tilting toward
my voice. I tell them, "easy, easy,"
as though I could calm a storm in
the trees. I have been so long moored
in the dark you cast in me, tell me
am I to know the fathoms of touch,
the terrain of a lover's body?

They whisk fly and dust
with their tails, one pushes her head
between my breasts. Lead me daily
to the waters of those brown
eyes. Let me go from the fear that
climbs me into sutures of prayer.

Sweat and hoof stomp—the prickle
and shed of a million particles. After
all that haunts me, I want to give you
No and *Enough already*. From the woods,
a chorus command of small sounds,
tenderfoot in the undergrowth. They
throw their heads as they leave.

Braid

To tie the shoelace my father
shows me tuck under, pull through,
and the bow my limbs let go in.

Go on, kiss, nuzzle the round curve
of my thigh. I won't startle like a deer in the road.
What good am I held under such waves—a girl again
—skinny, skulking girl with scuffed knees.

I paddle my boat out of thinking, make the bargain
to climb onto the island of your hips.

Go ahead, pull me up by my arms
and turn me over. My eyes snap open like a doll's.
Tuck me in, a sweet Sally in red velvet
with lace trim.

My father wraps the bow into loops.
I tug and tug, a country undoing
in me. Tell me how my fingers can
work this one loose.

III

Dear Reader

I, too, begin with one hundred judgments on the gravel roads
through childhood. I think I am my own absence

and go on confessing the vacancy. I fall asleep in a field
and become the weather over the field. I go everywhere with you

in mind. At Muir Beach, I watch dogs chase sticks into the surf
and the surf chasing the thin legs of dogs onto the beach.

I, too, think only one will obey, fed so easily from a porcelain bowl.
I look for sea lions and steamships. This is my West and my East Coast.

The blinding light of regret happens to me too. I, too, have many deaths
to report. I pray to St. Francis to take a few back. Many demigods

gather around my grief to siphon off verses and chapters.
I, too, expect the world to be broken so that I may have a place in it.

Then You Fled the Room

Take down the circus mobile hanging above the crib.
Pull the pink streamers from the ceiling beams.
You are no one's lullaby.

Hours zip up in the tap of the morphine switch.
Where they cut you out: the numb stapled crown
gauze-taped closed across my belly.

White walls pull me into space. The airy yellow
flowers of the curtain drift in on hospital breath.
The doctor flicks an index finger against my I.V. bag.

Take down the circus mobile hanging above the crib.
Pull the pink streamers from the ceiling beams.
You are no one's lullaby.

You were a religion of the nettle bed. I went to sleep.
I woke up bearing you like a fluted narcissus,
broken stem in my fist.

I bump along the rocks, a spinster in the rift now.
You've been counted out, my precious one
in the hospital crematorium.

Take down the circus mobile hanging above the crib.
Pull the pink streamers from the ceiling beams.
You are no one's lullaby.

Heart with Interior View

—Bodies Exhibition, NYC, May 2006

The heart has gone amniotic, light forced up through the glass
into the braid. No surge, no gushing, a silent devotional
of muscle and valve suspended in clear fluid.

I look down into the vessel. The sea was here
with breaking, with salt—a thrall to belly, backbone,
knot of elbow, rough of heel, legions of nerves—
cities of afterthought that burned and pleasured the whole.

The heart split like a persimmon, no longer able
to manipulate time, no goods to exchange
for living. I would trade the finest detail
of flesh singed and corroded with stillness
for a story. Let me dress the heart in frill and lace
and call her girl, child.

Clear, unsinkable bubbles float like pearls
in the tank. There is still a whole country of feeling
to kill off. Red night, what do you say of your cold altar
the tourists gather around?

Two Horses

Two horses make a thunder in the field.
From this particular distance: in a school bus
on the road. The chestnut throws her head
into the gray stallion's neck. Frozen grass chips
under hooves and the ground alters: green visible
patches of the field kicked from a winter's sleep.

A girl leaves her breath on the school bus window.
Axis of dark flesh against bright flesh makes
a monument: arcing necks, kicking hooves,
and the mare's pale mane flicking across his tongue.
The back is not free. Cold air flows out a crack
and nudges the girl's chin.

Heavy begets heavy in the field. The ground alters.
The bus shifts gears down. The distance within
this particular girl: breath on the window wedded
to the vast morning thaw. Her legs, her own back,
handed-down cotton dress: not free. Ambushed.
The cry alters, heavy, a thunder in her throat.

Hood

The shadow beneath the red hood
has quit my face. I need his white hiss of teeth
and pink tongue curling against his snout.

I tell him of the lamp-lit windows in the house,
and watch his black shoulders heave away
into the forest. He cuts the path
before me where the sky lays in puddles.

I lower the hood. I am curve, beak, braid.
Not a girl at all. Was there ever room
for childhood? The wind speaks around me;
the trees orchestrate. I lift the hood.

Desire culls me: a journey that will marry me
to his hollow until I am the whole hunger.

The Killed Rabbit

In its eye a convex universe:
the white sea of a cutting board,
the gray muffled fringe of a foot,
and the whiskered spikes converging

in there, intruding equally on one another;
a knowing endless with the moment
of the room. No longer able to look away,
or gaze past, or see into, yet obligated

by depth and light. Fixed with all
that is far-gone, distilled to believe
all at once in geographies,
electric with repeating the truth,

not blinking away from the ceiling fan's
blades, churning the steamy kitchen air,
renewed in the execution of being seen.
Then you chop the head off, overcome by

the need for disregard, to remember
the necessity of flesh and the crude jarrings
of meat being stripped down to a stasis of red;
the lean muscles of a runner and leaper exposed.

Its eye assumes a transfixed nature while gazing
at black plastic lining a bucket. Displaced
in all that is held there, vision
is in fact a reckless understanding.

Inside the Pleiades

—*After James Turrell's* Pleiades *Mattress Factory, Pittsburgh, PA*

I was the horror of my horrors,
standing inside the only room offered.
He asked, "Who are you?"
I said, "Who do you want me to be?"

A switch snapping in my chest, that I was
in the streets and pregnant at sixteen—
my father telling me each year anew

he was certain I would be. The horror
of my horrors not to reach my hand
toward the stranger in the artificial night. We laughed
and cackles erupted across the walls.

I was the horrors of my horrors when he left
along the carpeted ramp into a summer day.
I came up against all the dying that had wanted me

and found my birth hour: August 27, 1972,
a San Francisco morning, fog and delivery trucks.
Facts snatched me up, the night room whipping
their lost trajectory into space.

Spider

This morning I listen again for the spider
that crawled in my ear when I was fourteen,
to the web builder threading its low hum of leg hairs,
stroking nerves. The spider that maneuvering deeper,
traced vibrations in me.

The emergency nurse asking again
how many months pregnant I was,
but she'd got the wrong room, the wrong pain.
Later, she held a light in my inflamed canal
and laughed when the spider became clear.

She flooded my ear with purified water
and the spider spilled into a steel pan,
legs caught in yellow crystals, dead already
inside me. This old pain in its eight-legged harrowing
 erupts again on my eardrum. I am never alone.

Bull Frog

I feed its death to the water. My down in the creek mojo
with a stolen butter knife. A leg sprung from no rock.
A fatty jaw answered, tongue idling at current,
saying *bubble-pop* to air.

You want me to make a castle in the sand,
towers and tunnels gutted with a fist. Only this creature
and its stillness come to mind, how I open the belly
and split its cold terrain of eye-white skin.

I suspect love is like the water's trickle from a drainage pipe
at the pool's edge, never quite full of its seepage.

I work quickly while water-skaters make their black journey
over whatever the water closes on. I am fixed with all
the trinkets of stash: to keep a flat nostril separated from song.
You see my hands filled with the heart's digestible sound.

Unattended

Love a ribbon, love a kite tail, and love a feather
that has known its season on the wing. It's a prayer
I live far into this afternoon's song.

I want to ask if there is an origin for the scent,
a body for the bloom. I reach for her
and the consequence is

feeling. The curtain opens its floral arm
into the room. I call her birds onto my branches.
I slip my tongue in her curving.

My throat wrecked by all the not saying.
I will attend to an eternity of "I," knowing
I'm not hungry enough for this afternoon's psalm.

Sometimes Oranges

I want to throw them out, but they're
a bit of summer from somewhere.
Too late to slice them into eighths
or juice their thick skins; they've shriveled

and fermented into potpourri hulls
in the dry oil-heated air. They fetter
in their skins in the blue bowl
below the kitchen window.

No fruit flies lay eggs or ants arrive,
drawn by the sweet. No white derision
and green infusion of molds encouraged
by damp and warm; their carapaces

remind me that I forget to eat. My spoiled
American appetite has forgotten hunger,
the life I could spare to give up this jubilation
around the blue bowl.

Regarding Mercy

You will work for the zero of the throat
You will *not* get away with a better ending
You will be cremated with saying "I"
Your children will become third world countries
Your fury will be a white canoe in green water
You will weather a lone cloud in the Sierras
Your beliefs will seep from a cracked bowl
Your portrait will shut away the confession
You will worship the rubble, the ransack
You will fish for the split-tongued stamen
You will practice a lion's sleep
You will not be safe

IV

Prayer Found in Water Pouring
Down a Bus Window

You maker of glass. Bell-ringer.
Black-and-white cow sunk up to the knees
in an alfalfa field. Thunder of wheel
and spring. Rain on a tin roof. Particle of lint
crazy with drifting in the bus air. Bringer of the girl
across the aisle. Fastener of the red ribbons
knotting her hair. Keeper of all the words
that call you into being. Leaver of praise.
Crack that I may slip through

into my grief, fracturing with the likenesses
of truth. Awe that is my terror. You vagabond
of all the tides reeking their magic in the house of my eye.

Ultrasound Aubade

The doctor shows me a sepia mushroom,
a cancerous orchid, a tether ball winding
and winding a pole. You, a shadow
insisting pulse and blood, my shadow.

You're a lobster. You're an old, deflated inner tube.
You're the weather in a tornado, muscles
funneling debris. Nothing can

change you about: the thrashing salmon
swimming into my gut, the brown bear
pushing his nose into my ribs. Dead spaces
and a web of blood vessels converge.

I still feel like that child digging
a hole with a spoon to bury a sparrow—
its eyes eaten out by ants, not old enough
to mother anyone.

Cavity in the Rubenesque Façade

Lucid is a vein the nurse puts
the needle in. I am not sorry
for the sword. I pull and pull and
more bloody rope snakes to surface.

I never really wake; drugs come and go.
I dream I have a wound, big as
Aphrodite's shell. I have so many tongues
I can't keep them all! I say thanks
for the ship that sails across choppy waters

and lays me out on the surgeon's table,
a dumb girl blinking into operating room lights,
a visage of masked faces looking down
into my own. You see, a woman

is a bowl waiting for cups of rice,
or his car keys and candy bar wrappers.
A woman is round and floatable, buoyed
by her own excessive curves. The heart
monitor beeps endless for now.

I am blessed, finally released from
the hell that is rotten but not abstract
to their clamps and scalpels. Like old shards
from *Coors* bottles, you tip out of me.

April Spill-Off

The white-knit bonnet gulps at the surface.
Its ribbon ties swim tendrils out into leaves
and black water. A round head changes its mind,

sometimes egg, sometimes deflated
on a side. The fat tassel perched on the dome's
peak has a brown lip of stain.

Is this where my child has gone to sleep?
A bloated pearl headed for the sewer?
She has gotten so far from my body, dreamed of now

by many waves. A ghost in the gutter,
a plump angel awash with debris.
I can't just fish her out with a stick.

I follow the bonnet's ebb toward the narrowing
concrete walls, until she departs against the grill's teeth,
into still blacker water.

Parenting the Void

Cells transpire to become a child,
the flourishing edges of a minute beginning,
already embellished with a wardrobe
and a three-part name. I never make it

to umbilical joinings or a dimpled chin:
lost in a clandestine tide. I collapse into detail,
a reef that takes hours of writing
to transgress. And no attention is left

when I finally arrive at my apex:
the nursery rhymers chanting,
"once alone, once alone." I could be
sitting under a parachute's

great swelling dome in fifth grade,
my classmates lifting and dropping
the vibrant silk all around me,
red, blue, green, and visible seams

where the billowing shell grabs the air;
in their fists the world's skin until my turn
ends. My pen skids into blue margins.
What can I possibly write that might equal

a child's weight and warmth filling my arms?
I will call off the tide. I will fill pages.

Magician

To the conjurer of rabbits out of black hats, the escapist
down to his final act of vanishing beneath fifty pounds of chains,
you are born. To his legacy of tricks and Houdini-style
metamorphosis just waiting to spin out

into the San Francisco morning, where delivery trucks
back up to doors, caution lights sending yellow
like a heartbeat against the night.

He puts his hand over your mouth. Are you
the fire-eater? You come direct from the illusionist
to catapult from the black raft of his blessing.
The infant devotion: eyes newly open

believe the world: murky, against the white walls
ambient motions. You'll play a charmed rodent, and disappear
beneath his black cape. Another feat of possession.

Another vat of bottled smoke. He loosens knots,
saws the box open, rips a red scarf from his sleeve.
The silk becomes a dove becomes a rabbit
and the cages hide in the floor.

Bird Leaving a Branch

The days are ash. You lie down in the chalk outline.
You bring the favorite blue dress and drape its flood
over a chair. Dying is a beautiful dream, the propaganda
every heiress needs for her fortune of misery.

The pink and red geraniums in your window boxes survive.
The child that didn't choose you is air sending a dragonfly
to tap its fat green head on the windowpane, and rally memory.

The hound of regret has come for you.
The blur of a sentence you read in an obituary
draws you down the Styx on your torrential raft of worries.

Here is the umbrella you'll forget to take
when the storm comes on.

Meditation on Four West

Red tulips are against hospital policy.
Tuesday through Saturday I'm allowed
a cold cup of coffee with breakfast.
I am in the room between my ears.
I hear blueberry pie recipes and baseball
scores in the television static.

The candy striper yells, "Get your pills,
Get your pills!" the spokes clicking
in her cart wheels. Can I have
the pill for: I'll try not to kill myself
with the red tulips on the nightstand?

Time for confessions: when I am
among towering Victorians, I become a thief
of the trellis. My puppy eats the eyes
out of the teddy bear's face. I'll trade you
two fat blooms for the foghorn's distant cry.

About disease: It's no good inside the stout heart
of the colonizing cells; the blackness inside me
drinks, slaps cool waters into my throat,
and sucks air.

I've pulled the seam so far open on the past
I'll never get the dress closed.

From Her Lips to God's Ears

She spins the green apple on its waxy round side,
  starting and stopping its progress with slender fingers.
"You must want to be a mother?" she demands.
The toy, like a child's spinning top, she forgets
  and it whirls toward the black oak edge.

"Your apple," I say. And she turns to rescue
  this remaining chore from her breakfast.

When her eyes depart from mine, I stare into the yoke
  all saucy on my plate. I can't bear this brightness
so early in the day. My coffee black at the lip,
  I'd like a pair of mirror shades and a poker face.

"So you want children?" I inquire.
"God willing," she gasps and rolls the apple again,
  the waxy skin and polished wood never at rest,
    until her white smile when she bites into the whiter flesh.

Sunbathing

Through my eyelids the sun's red diamond
can't make me go blind, but I'm going to burn.
My thighs tingle until the pores sweating,
my throat thirsty again.

A tree ant appears on my arm
and when I go to swat him
disappears, until I accept his sometimes
getting lost on me.

The leaves turn the trees out,
pollen and spore energized toward escape.
My hearing spins after a motorcycle in highway traffic,
slingshots after an airplane with a choice of cities.

I am screwed back into the earth,
scorched in the grass. No childhood. No death.
Soon to be taken up by the business
of business, sucked back into the rush, colliding

with a whole angry world of needs. The ant tries again
to incorporate my shell laid across his path
and I split his body open with a fingernail.

Girl in the Woods

She is willing to be blamed, to wait out the dignity the earth restores
when a fern sword springs between her ribs, pushes its way through:

her last gesture. This, the richest soil! In the outer circumstance:
white sandals, a cotton hair tie, a flowered dress, a neat brown ponytail.

She does not have to make excuses—all her failings to produce pleasure
and exactness. Her body has magic left.

It is not a cruelty the way she is taken from herself: the root system forming,
the mosses growing fine denominations. Her neck bent so she is always

looking past a fallen birch trunk toward a duck pond. All these months
the birds have been singing to her, high whistles and twitters right into her ear,

so she might rise glorious from all that sleep and exclaim, "Where are you
my love?" Forgiveness is what she does best. Now there is no retort.

Now her eyes look through themselves and settle on the back of her skull
for that deep vision. Her landscape overwhelmed with restless clues,

enough to fill the palms, to fill the eyes with infinite tribulation.
It is herself, unsettled and chilly to approach, yellow tendons pulled taut,

keeping her together. The woods hum around her, ghost woods.

Hare in My Garden

The hare is all hind legs,
muscled and ready to spring
from my clutch. Mouth open,
long inward-pointing teeth
stained green and brown.
It cries, some screech I thought a bird.
I am the one who arrives.

Almost as big as my cat
and no wounds I can see except its heart
racing against my breast. Tells me again,
after all these years the rabbit's dying
I cannot bear.

I take it to the edge of the cottonwoods
and let it spring off my chest, out from my body;
its brown and gray coat settles back into its grain.

When I was six, I put my palms in the pelts
my father nailed to boards. I could not tell from death
the animal my fingers hassled.
I tried to want a lucky rabbit's foot,

but of all the rhythms I met against my breast
that rabbit's was the most insistent,
and what I learned was the heart and fear,
the heart and fear.

Pelvis with the Distance

In a desert, she woos air currents into a whistle.
She calls her child Windy and births clouds
and suckles dust. Everything passes, the
black hills behind her, the night before
her. Knowing this makes her osseous
and ligament-free, the joints long ago
released from aching flesh and blood
flow, like a pelican's wings clumsy
on dry earth. The sea has receded
some thousand miles. If the sky falls,
if the cattleman knocks his hard boot
on her tail bone, if the vultures hang about,
or the wire dipping between telephone poles
buzzes, the eye she is given does not look away.
Her wings almost come off the ground. In the dry
pockets, in the marrow's fine chambers, she remembers.

The Get Away

In April's accolade of green, I run a red trail
farther into its dirt. Pine needles blur
in the canopy, the sky in a puddle explodes

with me. I cannot be accountable for depth.
I breathe in and shadows fall under
the quickness of my feet. A stick snaps

and another runner plummets along the north trail,
also certain that here, *here* the transience
is spectral and determined by epiphany.

My jacket zipper makes cricket notes
against my stride. I am alone again. Inside,
the surprise is gone. What is coming will not be

comprehended. I can never catch its eye
around a tree. Breath is a dry pinch in
my throat. My ponytail flings cool sweaty tears

on my shoulders. I lose the trail and myself
only to find the rough leaping of a shadow;
the creature also makes its way through the forest,
a gait ceaseless and impossible to escape.

Biographical Note

Amber Flora Thomas is the recipient of several major poetry awards, including the Dylan Thomas American Poet Prize, Richard Peterson Prize, and Ann Stanford Prize. Her published work includes *Eye of Water: Poems* (University of Pittsburgh Press, 2005) which won the Cave Canem Prize. Most recently, her poetry has appeared in *Callaloo, Orion Magazine, Alaska Quarterly Review, American Literary Review, Southern Poetry Review,* and *Crab Orchard Review,* among other publications. She is a native of rural Northern California. She received her MFA from Washington University in St. Louis. Currently, she is an assistant professor of creative writing at the University of Alaska Fairbanks.